Let's Make Yogurt!

Let's Make Yogurt!

HERON
BOOKS

Published by
Heron Books, Inc.
20950 SW Rock Creek Road
Sheridan, OR 97378

heronbooks.com

Third Edition © 1976, 2021 Heron Books.
All Rights Reserved

ISBN: 978-0-89-739248-8

Printed in the USA

30 December 2021

LEARNING
at the
SPEED
of *You*

At Heron Books, we think learning should be engaging and fun. It should be hands-on and allow students to move at their own pace.

To facilitate this we have created a learning guide that will help any student progress through this book, chapter by chapter, with confidence and interest.

Get learning guides at
heronbooks.com/learningguides.

For teacher resources,
such as a final exam, email
teacherresources@heronbooks.com.

We would love to hear from you!
Email us at *feedback@heronbooks.com*.

IN THIS BOOK

Chapter 1

What Is Yogurt?

Chapter 1

What Is Yogurt?

Yogurt is a thick, soft food made by growing special things in milk. For over four thousand years, people have been making yogurt. It was popular long ago in countries like India, Israel and Egypt. It is still very popular today and is eaten in nearly all parts of the world.

WHAT'S GOOD ABOUT YOGURT?

First of all, it's easy to digest. This means it's easy for your stomach to break it down so it can be used by your body. When you drink a cup of milk, less than half of it is digested in the first hour. But if you eat a cup of yogurt, your stomach can digest nearly all of it in the same amount of time.

Yogurt is an especially healthy food. Besides being easy for your body to digest, it has protein and calcium, food substances that make your bones and teeth strong, and help your body grow well. There is another reason it is good for you that you'll find out about in the next chapter.

Another good thing about yogurt is that you can make it at home. And you can make yogurt that's plain, flavored, or even frozen!

Chapter 2

Bacteria

Chapter 2

Bacteria

Bacteria are tiny living things that are not plant or animal, but make up their own group. Some cause diseases, but many kinds are helpful. They are so small that it takes a microscope to see what they look like.

BACTERIA AND YOGURT

Helpful bacteria are used to change milk to yogurt. The bacteria causes the milk to get thicker and chunkier, and to become a bit tart, or sour tasting.

When changing milk to yogurt, bacteria break down some of the sugar that is in the milk and turn it into something called "lactic acid." This is what gives yogurt its tartness. Bacteria that make yogurt tart are also used to make other sour foods, like pickles, cheddar cheese and sauerkraut. If you have eaten any of these, you may notice that they have the same kind of sour or sharp taste.

Two or more kinds of special bacteria work together to make yogurt. One kind makes the milk tart and thick like custard or pudding. Another kind helps the first one do its job, but also gives the milk the "special" yogurt flavor.

BACTERIA IN YOUR BODY

Inside your stomach and intestines, the area in your body called the **gut**, there are about 100 trillion bacteria. There are hundreds of different types of bacteria in your gut. The good bacteria help protect your body from the harmful ones.

When everything is in good shape, there is a special balance in your gut bacteria that keeps you healthy. With this special balance, you have a lower chance of getting sick. You can also digest food better.

When the balance of your gut bacteria isn't right, it can cause all kinds of problems in different parts of your body.

Eating yogurt is a way to bring back the balance of gut bacteria when it's not doing well. In just an ounce of yogurt, there are about 1,000,000,000 helpful bacteria!

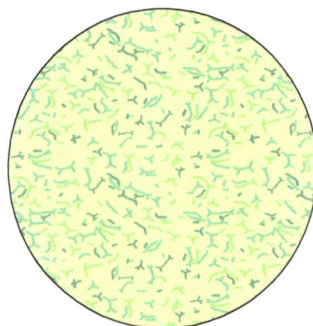

yogurt bacteria (in yogurt) under a microscope

Chapter 3
Things to Know

Chapter 3

Things to Know

HEAT AND YOGURT

Bacteria are everywhere around us. Some are good for us and some aren't. Bacteria comes from the soil and air and water. Any kind of fresh food has some bacteria present. Warm animals, like cows and even people, have lots of bacteria living on them. Milk has some bacteria in it from cows and other places.

For food to be heathy, it shouldn't have too many bacteria.

When we make yogurt, our first step is to heat the milk *hot* to kill bacteria that are already in the milk. But we don't boil the milk because that might spoil its taste.

We cool the milk some, add helpful yogurt bacteria, and keep the milk *warm* to help the yogurt bacteria grow. If we heat the milk right, nearly all the bacteria growing are helpful yogurt bacteria, not bacteria from the cow or soil or air.

Yogurt bacteria grow best at about 110°F, which is a little warmer than the temperature of the human body. They will grow some at lower temperatures (even in the refrigerator, although very slowly) but they like about 110°F best.

Interesting Fact: You may have heard a nursery rhyme about a child eating curds and whey. But what are they? Yogurt bacteria make the solid part of the milk (called **curd**) settle out, leaving the liquid part (called **whey**) on top. Yogurt is the thickened curd that you eat. After the curd and whey separate, you can throw away the whey or drink it. Whey has lots of minerals that are good for your body.

YOGURT STARTER CULTURES

A **culture** is a group of bacteria that someone grows on purpose to do a certain thing. A **starter** or **starter culture** is one that is used to change the qualities of foods and give them interesting tastes.

For example, starter cultures are used to turn milk into cheese, to turn grape juice into wine, and to make bread rise. A **yogurt starter culture** is a group of bacteria used to turn milk into yogurt.

Once you've made some yogurt, you can then use it as a starter culture to make more yogurt. But you always want to make sure you have a pure starter culture with the correct kinds of bacteria. If too many of the wrong bacteria are left in the milk or get into the starter, it will not make good yogurt. Then you will have to throw it away and get a fresh starter culture.

The easiest way to get started is to buy a small container of plain yogurt from a store and use it for your starter culture.

KEEPING OUT BAD BACTERIA

Your yogurt will be spoiled if bad bacteria gets into it. Here are ways to keep out bad bacteria.

When you use store yogurt for your starter culture, don't use it for anything else. Be sure to keep the container as clean as possible, and use only clean utensils when you take out some of the yogurt. Don't open the container any more than you have to.

Never put a spoon into the yogurt that you have already put in your mouth. When you put that spoon into the yogurt, you add millions of mouth bacteria to the yogurt. They might grow and completely spoil the starter culture or any new yogurt you make!

SAFETY NOTE

When you make your yogurt, it is important to use only kitchen dishes and spoons that are used for food preparation.

IF IT DOESN'T WORK EVERY TIME

As many cooks will tell you, anything they make will turn out a little differently each time, even when they do all the steps the same way. If you've cooked other things yourself, you may have noticed this.

So don't worry if your yogurt doesn't come out exactly right every time. Just try again!

Chapter 4

Two Parts to Making Yogurt

Chapter 4

Two Parts to Making Yogurt

It is helpful to remember that there are two parts to making a batch of yogurt.

- The first part is called *preparation*. As part of this step, you heat the milk to kill unwanted bacteria, cool the milk and then add yogurt bacteria with your starter culture.

- The second part is called *incubation*. **Incubate** means to keep something living in a way that will make it grow. For example, a hen incubates eggs by sitting on them to keep them warm and make them hatch into chicks. When you make yogurt, incubation involves keeping the milk at the right temperature so the yogurt bacteria can grow and turn the milk into yogurt.

Now you're ready to make some yogurt!

Let's Do This!
Plain Yogurt

For this activity you will need

- a clean 1-pint jar and lid
- a 9-10 quart, hard-sided cooler
- measuring cup
- tablespoon
- hot water bottle
- two bath towels
- pot holder
- 1 cup of milk
- packet of powdered milk
- a small, unopened container of high-quality, plain yogurt with live yogurt bacteria. The label should say "active cultures."
- pan
- optional: a digital candy thermometer

Steps

Preparation

1. Measure out 1 cup of milk and pour it into the pint jar.

2. Add 3 tablespoons of powdered milk and stir until it dissolves.

3. Heat the jar of milk in a pan of water until the jar is too hot to hold, but don't boil the milk. If you're using a thermometer, get the temperature to approximately 180° to 190°. Heat a tablespoon in the water at the same time.

4. Once the milk is hot enough, carefully remove the jar from the water with a pot holder and set it on a wire rack or a towel to cool. (Putting it directly on a cool surface could cause the jar to crack; using a towel or rack keeps this from happening.)

5. Check the jar from time to time to see how much it has cooled off. When it is barely cool enough to keep against your face, go on to the next step. If you are using a thermometer, the milk should be about 110°.

6. Add the starter culture. With the tablespoon that you heated, measure out 1 tablespoon of yogurt. Stir the yogurt into the milk you heated. Then screw the top back on the jar.

Incubation

Important Tip: Do not stir the yogurt after it begins to thicken. If you do, it may stop thickening and end up soupy.

1. Line the cooler with a folded bath towel. It should go across the bottom and up the sides of the cooler.

2. Fill the hot water bottle with very hot tap water.

3. Place the hot water bottle in the cooler and put your jar of yogurt on top of it.

4. Fold the bath towel over the hot water bottle and yogurt jar.

5. Put the other folded bath towel on top, and then put the lid on the cooler.

6. Incubate the jar for at least 6 hours. After 6 hours, check to see if it is thickening. Don't shake or stir the jar as that will keep the yogurt from thickening.

7. If your yogurt has thickened, put it in the refrigerator. When it is cold, it will be firmer and ready to eat. Remember the whey you read about earlier? If there is any whey on top, you can pour it off. Or you can keep it to use in other recipes.

8. No matter how your batch of yogurt turns out, keep it for the next activity.

9. Wash everything you are done with. Unless you are going to make more yogurt today, put everything away.

Chapter 5
Tips for Success

Chapter 5

Tips for Success

When making yogurt, the main thing to keep in mind is that if the yogurt bacteria get too hot, most of them may die. And if they get too cool, they won't grow enough to turn the milk into yogurt.

Most problems come from not following the directions carefully.

Here are some problems you could run into and suggestions for what to do.

Problem 1: *The mixture smells and tastes like yogurt but it isn't thick enough.*

The yogurt made from the recipes in this book won't be very thick, but they should at least be jelly-like. If you stir or shake the yogurt too soon, it may stop thickening.

What to do: Make up another batch but do not stir or shake the yogurt after it begins to thicken.

Or add a thickener such as milk powder to your yogurt batch and continue incubating it until it begins to thicken. Then refrigerate it. Directions for this are given in the next chapter.

Problem 2: *The mixture is still liquid like milk. It might smell like milk or yogurt.*

There could be several reasons for this:

- there weren't enough yogurt bacteria to start with,
- the yogurt bacteria were killed, or
- the yogurt bacteria didn't grow enough to turn the milk into yogurt.

What to do: You still may be able to make it into a good batch of yogurt. Stir in more starter culture, and re-incubate the jar at the right temperature until the yogurt begins to thicken. Don't let the jar get too hot as the high temperature can kill the yogurt bacteria. Then refrigerate the yogurt.

Problem 3: *The mixture doesn't smell or look right or it has bubbles in it. It doesn't smell like yogurt (and it might not taste right either!).*

Here are some ways this might happen:

- Too many outside bacteria were able to get into the milk jar. The milk, container and utensils must be heated to kill unwanted bacteria or they will grow in the warm milk. And care must be taken not to let a lot of bacteria from the air (or the table, your hands, or your mouth) get into the warm milk because they will grow, too.

- Too many outside bacteria got into the milk and then the milk jar wasn't kept warm enough for the yogurt bacteria to grow well, so the outside bacteria took over.

- Your starter culture didn't have enough good yogurt bacteria in it, and the wrong kind of bacteria took over. This usually doesn't happen unless your starter culture was very old and other bacteria grew in the starter. Or the starter you used didn't have "active cultures" as called for in the recipe.

- The jar was heated too hot and it killed off the yogurt bacteria, plus other bacteria was let in (such as by using a dirty spoon).

What to do: Don't eat it. Throw it out. There are too many of the wrong kind of bacteria growing in it and it is not healthy to eat.

Start again with a fresh starter culture. Do not reuse any jars or spoons without washing them first in a dishwasher or heating in very hot or boiling water to kill off the unwanted bacteria.

Let's Do This!
Troubleshoot Your Yogurt

To do this activity, you will need

- The batch of yogurt you made in the last activity.

Steps

1. Look at the batch of yogurt you made, and taste it if you want to. If it is good enough to eat, you do not have to do anything, and you are done with this activity! (Remember that this yogurt will not be as thick as store yogurt.)

2. If the yogurt is not good enough to eat, continue with the rest of the steps.

3. Decide which of Problems 1 through 3 in Chapter 5 fits your situation.

4. Decide what you should do to make the yogurt edible. It may be necessary for you to make a new batch of yogurt and to follow the steps more carefully.

5. Go over your plan with your teacher. Then do it.

6. Wash everything you are done with. Unless you are going to make more yogurt today, put everything away.

Chapter 6
Let's Get Fancy!

Chapter 6

Let's Get Fancy!

Once you have mastered the skill of making plain yogurt, you can get fancy!

An easy way to make your yogurt fancier is by adding fruit. You can use the recipe in this book.

But there are many other things you can do with yogurt.

Try adding your yogurt to a fruit smoothie.

Make a yogurt parfait—layers of yogurt, granola and fruit.

Or on a hot day, try mixing in smashed fruits and honey, then freezing your yogurt in popsicle molds for a cold treat.

Your imagination is the limit!

Let's Do This!
Fruit Yogurt

This recipe makes more than 1 cup (8 oz.) of yogurt.

If you want to make a larger batch of yogurt, you can use a quart jar and double the amounts of all the ingredients (milk, yogurt starter, powdered milk, fruit filling). The preparation and incubation are done the same way.

For this activity you will need

- a clean 1-pint jar (16 oz.) with lid
- a 9-10 quart, hard-sided cooler
- measuring cup
- tablespoon
- hot water bottle
- two bath towels
- pot holder
- 1 cup of milk
- packet of powdered milk
- a small, unopened container of high-quality, plain yogurt with live yogurt bacteria. The label should say "active cultures."
- about ¼ cup (3 to 5 tablespoons) fruit filling. (See note below.)
- pan
- optional: a digital candy thermometer

Note:

For fruit filling, jam or smashed berries can be used. If the berries are especially juicy, you may want to pour some of the juice off. Too much juice can make the yogurt runny.

Canned pie filling makes great fruit yogurt, but each can has more filling than you will use in one batch of yogurt. The extra pie filling can be kept in a refrigerator for a little while for future use.

A small jar of toddler fruit dessert works well and is the right amount for one cup of yogurt. Be sure to use fruit dessert, not strained fruit for toddlers, as the strained fruit has too much liquid.

Steps

Preparation

1. Measure out 1 cup of milk and pour it into the pint jar.

2. Add 3 tablespoons of powdered milk and stir until it dissolves.

3. Heat the jar of milk in a pan of water until the jar is too hot to hold, but don't boil the milk. If you're using a thermometer, get the temperature to approximately 180° to 190°. Heat a tablespoon in the water at the same time.

4. Once the milk is hot enough, carefully remove the jar from the water with a pot holder and set it on a wire rack or a towel to cool. (Putting it directly on a cool surface could cause the jar to crack; using a towel or rack keeps this from happening.)

5. Check the jar from time to time to see how much it has cooled off. When it is barely cool enough to keep against your face, go on to the next step. If you are using a thermometer, the milk should be about 110°.

6. Add the starter culture. With the tablespoon that you heated, measure out 1 tablespoon of yogurt. Stir the yogurt into the milk you heated. Then screw the top back on the jar.

Incubation

Important Tip: Do not stir the yogurt after it begins to thicken. If you do, it may stop thickening and end up soupy.

1. Line the cooler with a folded bath towel. It should go across the bottom and up the sides of the cooler.

2. Fill the hot water bottle with very hot tap water.

3. Place the hot water bottle in the cooler and put your jar of yogurt on top of it.

4. Fold the bath towel over the hot water bottle and yogurt jar.

5. Put the other folded bath towel on top, and then put the lid on the cooler.

6. Incubate the jar for at least 6 hours. After 6 hours, check to see if it is thickening. Don't shake or stir the jar as that will keep the yogurt from thickening.

7. If your yogurt has thickened, put it in the refrigerator. When it is cold, it will be firmer and ready to eat.

8. After the yogurt has cooled, pour off the whey and stir in the fruit filling.

9. At this point, you can also add any sweetener you like.

10. Eat your yogurt, and share it with others if you like!

11. Wash everything and put it away.